La Fin du Monde

La Fin
du
Monde

Poems

Chris Ryan Lauer

RAMBOUILLET PRESS

©2022 Rambouillet Press
www.RambouilletPress.com

This book was set in Cochin and Garamond Premier Pro
by Rambouillet Press.
Printed and bound in the United States of America.

ISBN: 979-8-218-01792-7

CONTENTS

La Fin du Monde

Epilogue

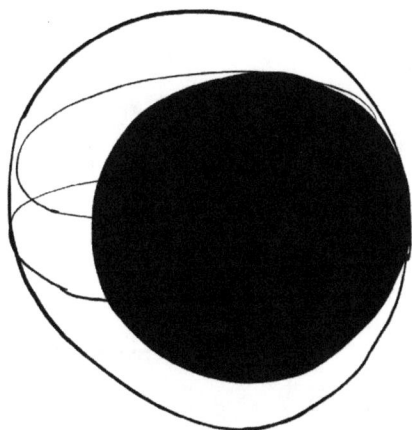

Chapter One

I ONLY WANT THE SUN

I WELCOME INTRUSIONS LIKE THE SUN

too much
gin
but you're the only truth in my cup
i'll be sleeping with you sometime between now
and next week
      you'll tell the world
      that i'm a genius
      and we'll repeat it now
      and again
      on this spanish earth

WE'LL HAVE EVERYTHING OR NOTHING

light showers
      lavender
            petrichor

gevrey chambertin

a face out of
gazette du bon ton

i'd love it if we made it

WHEN THE HANDS COME DOWN

bonal &
soda
peeled orange

sundressed
underneath the
cirrus clouds
she reads to me from the new yorker
& tells me   *i love you*

there's nothing left to do now
but unpack

THE COUNTRY GOES BY AS NONSENSE

blanc doux
36,000 feet
a rarity of complete lulls
you read me the life of borodin

i can only sleep with a dark cloth over my eyes too

■

A RESPITE FROM

overindulged
                    in bourgueil
the sky is grey

            fleeting sun spells

bra off
underneath
                    you

reading
            le monde

I HAVE LOOKED ALMOST HALF A CENTURY

convoluted & juvenile
yet you laugh at my jokes

love
the way that i look
at you

within this sphere of trembling temporality
i tie a single windsor
as you study me from 7 below

remember that i'm a man
not a communist regime

WITHOUT SUBTERFUGE

i do not create my emotions
i participate in life   &   love

freshly &
without concept

      & allow the simultaneity of its
      beauty

WHEN TOMATOES ARE RIPE

eyes bigger than stomach

 flexible
        going away occasionally
but not too far

form becomes a dream
an impression
        left upon the retina
                with thoughts that have no apparent basis in inference

all that i see
belongs to me

PORTA ROSSA

love in the afternoon
a room with a view
        i take a photograph of you
braless
        eyes on me
lying down by the edge
you have the fever now

BOIS DE BALINCOURT

saturday morning
white linen sheets

maison no.4
bois de balincourt

i rub off on you

A POEM IS A NAKED PERSON

the infraordinary
  the humdrum

nude
afternoon congression
  a moment without a proper name

i know where i'm going

■

I ONLY WANT THE SUN

the world around residency
french modernism
requires sections
on display
at the met
and in our bedroom

TULIPS   .

sunday morning
rain on the windows
slightly opened
the smell of fresh tulips
in bed with you
& the dog

DUNE

walking along anacapa
hand in hand
caffeinated
cafuné

bougainvillea spectabilis sits on its pedestal

PLUM

wake up walk up 1st

oxblow
cortado
&   anatomy

clos du val
in the afternoon

IN THE CORNERS OF FRONT YARDS

madrona
        dusk
on the porch
you   me
        &   jack herrer
discussions about
nothing
        everything

THANKS BE TO STRAUSS

i appreciate the drive over the bridge
into marin
more than any other

i picture us living here
someday

raising a daughter together

we'll have a small family

a good one

you hold onto the back of my hand

giant steps are what you take

i play the the police
as i continue along through the fog

MONTLAKE EGGO

i fry an egg

the edges are slightly charred
black

sea salt
pink
      yolk intact

i place it over a slice
of grand central
& avocado

i always get it right the first time

i'm real fuckin liberal
          with the butter

UNNAMED ENTITY

an unstable presence
i'm learning to love you
more

i make up a song
to score the
images in mind

a dissonant harmony

becomes a forty part
motet

AS LONG AS THE SUN LASTS

i'll have
you
&
you'll have me

as long as
the sun lasts

Chapter Two

LOVE IS TRANSIENT

A HALL WITHOUT FOOTSTEPS

the prospect of your proposition
an offering of stability
stretching indefinitely before me
is hemming me in
cutting me off
and i want to flee

I SAID LOVE IS TRANSIENT

romantically contorted
beings & things

entirely realistic
yet supernatural

our lives turn into   burning fevers

and we hide ourselves in the places where we find provisional truths

IN PROVENCE

inspired &
with undeterred momentum

but everything is waiting like the english
or a senior for their prescription to be filled
before the pharmacist arrives

        &
        everything wants
        more than it gives

        intrusively
        with large
        ungloved hands
                covered in cake

CHALKING UP NARRATIVES

litany
in the living room
art
life
         nocturnes
a discussion of what we anticipate
becoming

in front of me
my words flowing
through thin air
hear my story

i'm a member of the quiet hour
a sculpture of the 1980's

who drinks apéritifs
&
works out grief in a scandi
next to the xerographica
&
a broken fireplace

SAUVE QUI PEUT (LA VIE)

every man for himself
it's 6:07 am
i can accomplish everything
but most likely some things
i'm not interested in
scrolling
or
the news
instead i bathe with the door open
and discuss currency with myself
i'm alive once again

&

the scent of lavendula
inspires me to fuck you once more

i walk down to the kitchen
to eat a fried egg on a baguette
with avocado
bacon & microgreens
i think about how self involved i can be
and how sadly
it makes me
successful
appealing
blissful
i don't want to be a father to that

i see my reflection on the screen of my phone
while taking a sip of tea

the sound of cartoons
become invasive

i'm interested in viewing the
impressionist pieces from the
bemberg foundation

perfect

we'll start there

PERPETUAL ATERMOIENTS

living according to graphs

barefoot
          standing in honey   mizpah

perpetual atermoients

THE LEAVES YOU WALK UPON

queen anne
      books
      &
short lattes
      expressing itself as a continuum
i don't need to live with you
you're fine ink
forever
 in my new & selected poems
      spend time with
          me
      miss something now
think about that
      let's walk
there are too many one ways
      &
 do not enters in this city
      it forces me to follow a straight line
                        out of sight

I LET MY HEART GIVE OUT

self proclaimed virtuous ideals
unrealistic
       &&
pseudo sentimental

love turns me into an uneaten pear
and you into an ingenue
       washed up debutante

explosions
faces filled with smoke
we avoid our destiny

a heroine you no longer appear
i disappear

       into the crowd

a scientific gaze
and the permission to carry something
anything
out

ROMANCE OR THE END

a non descriptive utterance
performative

left unattended

a shattered highball

& the
      grain of my voice

TRIED TO SEW THE PARTS BACK ON

esprit de l'escalier

plodding upstairs

internal chortle

second floor   eristic

      one   aristocratic

MY HANDS LET GO

montlake
        damp

promises of human life

a broken oath

windows closing
        chugging denial
        only
                at first
but   able
        to shut the door when i use the bath now
i'm free
                available
        people unknown

it's 2:30 am
you're up
wishing i was the bottle
                darling

A PASS ON RUE BONAPARTE

i shower alone
      with her
in charcoal mines

and the laundry does itself

      the kind of pass where quarters end up
within me
      a profound attachment to myself

Chapter Three

LIMINAL SPACES

THERE IS NO PROMISE IN THE OTHER

we'll call it a draw
draw my ass   goddamn it
i won

suddenly it was my time
a resolution by god
the caves of the sea
hold me now
            after it all
                i figured i'd stay catholic
                        why jinks things

you never really know
what you're fighting for love
until you lose

I WOULDN'T CALL MY RUMINATIONS POETIC
BUT YOU SHOULD

discovering coffee at jayde's
while writing you

i was never awarded for anything
but should have been
for my battles won overseas
a navy ribbon or a crimson emblem
                given to me by your mother
flowers

the night ends & begins again

AWAY FROM THE EASEL

i'm a balloon in the air of dangerous glamour
what's to become of me
god has no clock
on the seventh day he stepped away from the easel
to push abstraction in new directions

there's not a whole lot of stability underneath his heaven

so i write from dreams down here
and speculate about tomorrow

THE WOMAN WHO THINKS SHE'S CHRIST

true colors
profiles for validation
sex
      money
                        feelings
              die
in the end
no longer   young
                   disappearing

away from home now
       &
       facing the
              pitfalls
              associated with
        a sophomore effort

RIPENESS CORRUPTS EVERY TREE

there will always be laws
and people to break them
the spring is the most dangerous season of the year

      cherry blossoms
      tulips
      rhododendrons basking in admiration
      sun shining
            while

i

      live here amongst them
above all else
      in this latter place

able to properly judge
      because of the inferior
      neighboring works
and   because
      only

i know how to solve you

HANG YOUR MEMORY OF ME AT THE LOUVRE

occupied
indifferent
accompanied
hurried
hesitant
alone

i   was

                  once

there

INTERIORS

life in a tall tower built by emery
isn't what it seems
everything is camouflage
everyone hates something there
      left behind on the upper west side
      with a green brick in my shoulder bag
          i'm a prophet now
          selling an inactive cryptocurrency
that attempts a come back each year
i can do anything   really
can i get a witness
or a better memory of it   all
like i have of my childhood in maryland
where the birds are bright orange
but the sky is grey by 4

ME AND YOU AND EVERYONE WE KNOW

when you said i love you for the first time
i responded by telling you
that i already have plenty of enemies

i'm used to it

i hail taxis by myself
like a thief

we were only together
in the headlines
our picture was on the front page

people talk about us now

we're an example

i've no envelope and don't know
how to send you this letter

COMPANIONS IN SOLITUDE

companions in solitude
with the latest woman
behind the camera
& a bottle of gin

there's enterprise
in good conversation
& waking up nude

A MUSE ALWAYS PRIES

i'd rather do it for you
than bask on the rampart
of some accomplishment
or undertake a new epic
to cling in wonderment to

of course you actually have to take the medicine
you're the one who taught me that
i wasn't mistaken

in this world
when you find a good place
you don't leave it

LIMINAL SPACES

bonal
ham & gruyère
on a baguette
with maille
for
le brunch

everything is a story
even the truth
    what's more authentic
    sex as medicine
    or
    "love" at the end of the world

        god
        you take a photograph of the sun and hold it above my head each day
        have a chat with me

    i love you
    are you wearing your robe

i read for revelation
i fuck for ~~validation~~   gratification
i write for keeps
i lie to exit
i smile when i'm praised
i laugh when the cubs lose
i cry over nothing
i live for myself

i feel everything
i can't absolve myself from wanting

A RETROSPECTIVE

i was much too formidable

you find company in
drones

& masquerade as a populist now

a clever, yet bogus, subterfuge

THE RESOLUTE URGENCY OF NOW

the scope of the genre
became too complex
to survive within
          i avoided suffering the same pitfalls
                    as the predecessors

the theatre applauds

i become
          myself

not a moissanite reduction
          or a restless french press
                    with purple sex opened up on the coffee table

BULL MARKET

& inconsistent
inconsequential
       sophomoric
              &
                              contrived
               transactional affair

the inevitable demise
delayed   by   gratification
the   night
before the trade deadline

SUSPENSION OF DISBELIEF

nothing is so humble
between the still and moving image
i fool the machine
histories keeps me awake at night
to reconsider those seemingly familiar settings
of
i   you   we
but
i'm a writer
i use people for what i write
is the story i'm told

A FLAW IN THE ROMANTIC IMAGINATION

the
        resistance

of
        the
                heart   wall   varies

depending
                on
        the
                place   where   you

        drive
                        in   the

                nail

LOVE IS COLDER THAN DEATH

i still ruminate

i'm afraid to forget your face

THE FACADE COMMISSION

in the spring
at
the crossroads
    of ongoing
    pivotal turns
        a bricktop shape of her
        is now high art for the community
        the facade commission
        rewards me for
        my aesthetic splendor
            of
        pictures revisited
            a true form
            tits out
            masterpiece

FREEDOM TRAIL

a historical rebellion
		bostonian

i realize my full potential

a revolution of the mind   occurs
a refusal to assent

self indulgence becomes   the   treatment

Chapter Four

AN APOLAUSTIC STRATEGY

AN APOLAUSTIC STRATEGY

my medicine
an attempt at exhausting
people
        places
becomes an
exercise in style
a retelling of the same story

A NEW ENGLAND DOCUMENT

i took a stranger to maine in october
i didn't know her well
but i'm a man escaped
from a life of sugarcoated arsenic

ELEVATOR TO THE GALLOWS

hans wegner
wishbone

tajarin
con
burro
e
salvia

a short glass of   larsonie
underberg
      bourbon

         orgeat
and   a fat fucking
lemon burn

ice cold
      low   brow
larceny

i reflect on my own
infidelities and
consider the notion that   nevertheless

i loved you

we are our own demons

POPES DO NOT MARRY

it's the end of vintage
abbia nóva
a
zev
rovine
        selection

senzavandalismi

a true pacific natural
at home

i've got a big bowl of ruffage
on my lap
&
i sit here under the eternal sun
that i created

a blackbird
with a fat fucking
worm

// the pendulum swings in my favor

WAR RUNS ON RUMORS

blue eyed wide
alive here in my own private maine
relevant & unweathered
      in
love triangles
      squares
              pentagons
lillies q eastern stained
on my white oxford
      drunk on the nose of dark diplomatico
      i'm one hell of a war tourist
      envy me for my own unique capabilities
      &
      shortcomings
              belch

MISSION DOLORES

60° sunny
full capacity
maskless parishioners
discussing high art & drinking rum
in coconuts with their heads sliced off
on an oversized blanket
next to the komondor
who has a perpetual smile & hair bun

the dealer
said he'll be exhibiting his
art at the university of notre dame
in the fall

i don't believe him

i have a contact high
&
i'm drunk

i sing along to
last ones left

BELIEVING SECRETLY THAT I WOULD BE THE ONE PERSON IN THE HISTORY OF MAN WHO WOULD LIVE FOREVER

elizabeth street
where
several women in shades of green
resemble eva
but i sleep next to others now
and the upper crust of this city pay them all white salary
  it's important to be in love most of the time
  all of the time
or in something that closely resembles it
  i find myself sleeping and waking everyday without an instruction manual
  and the postal van that's parked in front of my mailbox
    is the enemy
i think through conflicted feelings
involving
contrived intimacy
and a lack of authenticity
but coffee
  &
the opening of my soap glazed shower door
  allows the light to come in each morning
there's still one cloud left over my home
but i don't pay much attention to it
because i live in its interior
where a manic scene
  of wine
  laughter & gesticulation
  within a certain vacuous civilization intersect
each night

THE CONTEXT OF ST. IVES

it was a
fine rain
            drizzle
outside
at the opening of
strange attractors

warm in
a herringbone coat

the context of st. ives
an important point of inspiration

the PARIS REVIEW

i lose myself in the city
my ideas come to me in the streets
where i walk on water   in black suede lace ups
the crowd is a sea that invigorates my wandering mind
i sail in solitary
and am content
to be carried by the current

GOD FORGIVES...I DON'T

take a chance
and breathe the same air
as i do
        it's better
when i don't   cheat

i'm here   today   as   a   gentleman
drinking my tea in the back of the beatrice
while
admiring the aesthetics of sara in milan
        a crime has been committed but
        we are not dealing with law
christ   himself
can forgive sinners
but i don't
absolve false gods
only myself from blame   guilt
complicity
                however
                i   fear
        i fear becoming too familiar
                &
        breeding contempt
        so i hide myself in a dining room
        with a zebra on the wall
        and celebrate my life as an animal

FORM WITHOUT CONTENT

a manifestation of falsities
i exhibit connivance
for the ticket home
drink with me at the maybourne
write with me at the atelier
&
climb my copper ladder to the roof
      you'll look up to me forever from afar
      my brainy symmetric partner

on the move
first stop   gloster
for soft touch   tuck dust

no sense of proportions
bound in calculations
but there's nothing left to decide anymore
there's nowhere else
my long list of amenities
and jar of nuances
are now a linguistic memory

THE TOREADOR

advantageous in
sensation seeking
while sharing a home with subclinical symptoms
i escape to find fulfillment in
pillow-talk
      jargon

everything
& everyone   turns into writing
down here

     afternoon walks in the canyons

     no longer sitting nude damp
     under the hunter green trees
     talking big promises of emptiness

i remain calm under the influence
& pressure
like a toreador in crimson red
in a histrionic spring
by sharing fiction in exchange for an exit strategy

PICTURE & PROCESS

cordials
& bucatini
al vino al vino
i devour the entire
picture & process

I'LL SHARE MY ELECTIVE AFFINITIES

roblar
santa ynez

here for the clout
       bicycles
       &
       sémillon

NORI & TROUT ROE

south beverly
laker hoops
revolver
          the fury
nori &
trout roe

VIEUX CARRE

south beverly
re:find
fresh grapes
luca malbec
crispy duck roll
&
vieux carre

NORTH OF MONTANA

hunched over avocado bowl
persol
        sun in my eyes
& maria
back from madrid
with a fuck me frown on her face

APRILE

gjelina
sunday
half dozen   snow island (ME)

hand cut frites
birds of passage

an uncompromising presence   rooftop

the rightness of
these shifts of space

LOWER TOPANGA

freelander cab
venice beach wines

art from the confinement
on display in marcy's bungalow

she went down on me
before we fucked

i feared the ravine in her backyard

ART LUST LOVE

me me me
hurried
an excerpt from terminal boredom
a self critical biography
conscious drama
why why why

she's just fine though

my muse plays tennis with me
my muse cooks for me
my muse watches french cinema with me
my muse wakes me up in the morning with a kiss on the cheek
etc.
etc.

PASTOURELLE

end of mass

£10

      classic manhattan

      la roi de pierres

      opus one

tate swivel as my pulpit
celebrating
      an instinctive allegiance
      to myself

STRAIGHT UP RAW FRESH MACADAMIA

found niche at the robertson house

the unexpected florist   in her 87 will clark orange & black
drinking matcha for the day time buzz without the crash

drop ins   from harvard
direct to beverly hills

i've never eaten a turnip before
they're bland

i was living before   but now
it just hits different

ok
          but

aren't you glad
you're here with me instead

          was the response
when i told her
          i've always been more of a new yorker

EVERYBODY TRIES HARD BUT THE GODS

first sought out in tucson
dressed in newspaper
to becoming the only major statement in los angeles
who resurrects on easter

everything begins to flow gratuitously
melodic signs of mediterranean eyes smile in the sun
and the polytonic breeze in the open air of the warmth
gathers in the hills
     films become poems here
     conversation is music
          & the gifted holy bible is a currency used to purchase more sins
     of lust   vainglory

NEPÉTA

seer   &   scene
on waverly place
babbo
tajarin with butter & sage
wild arugula
nepèta sicily
discussions about the mets

the image has the last word

THE YEAR OF THE OX

lying in the reeds
to redemption on andalusia
      the year of the ox
back in the airy daylight
this swooped transition on the eyelids of the sea
bathing on its lips
to stay current
walking is no longer
        dry
              hurried
                    &&
                    perilous

LA FIN DU MONDE

1:01 friday
le bowl
la fin du monde
grey in l.a.
lo fi
75 porsche scenario
      paige   altering   devotion
      builds these
      poems for me
i marry the image of you
waiting at the bar
beige wrapcoat
red lips
an urgent sound of horns are audible

Chapter Five

YOUR LOVE COMES RUNNING BACK OUT OF THE BUSHES

LINEN LINE

like notes in the margin
on linen paper

   i pass through this ordeal
   with a modernist perspective

     &
      i feel

      graced by the powder of that view

YOUR LOVE COMES RUNNING BACK OUT OF THE BUSHES

nude in the guise of a myth
       no longer ruminating on ruins
sensing the unseen
the view from here has
become a museum inside my camera
the picture is   high art
that transcends everyday preoccupations

ON THE SIDE OF THE EIGER

miles & miles
down the autobahn
perched
on the side of the eiger

     i'm the ram

snow

     reigning

AUTONOMY AOSTA

alpe lys
on
rocks

adopted by the sun
i'm the last tycoon
shining again //
_____ a trillion watts

ONLY UNFULFILLED LOVE CAN BE ROMANTIC

it's been __ months
since i promised
      & failed
to save the day

you've been waiting in the rain outside of the
opera

i told you to wait
      & that pineapples are a sign
            of my second coming

i
am
indefectibly
myself

i exist in
a regime of too much
or not enough

my desire
is unwilling
to stop
at a
wrong

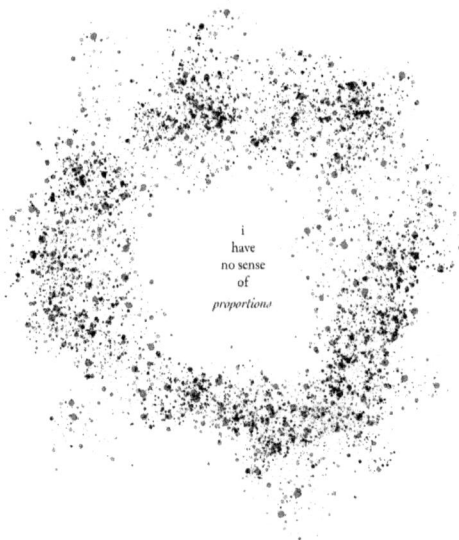

i
have
no sense
of
proportions

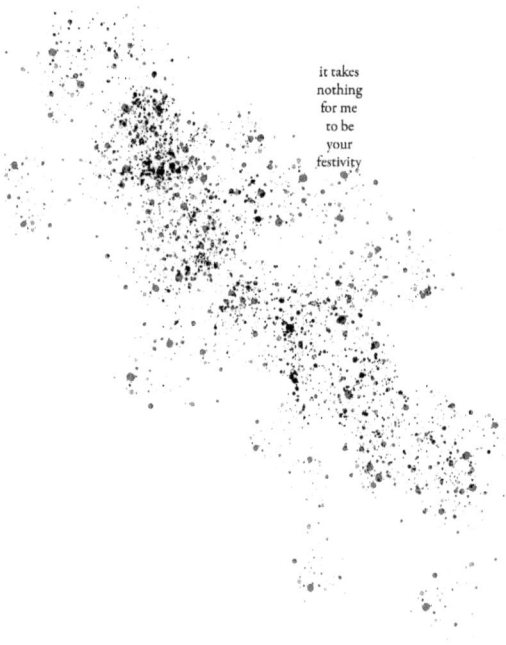

it takes
nothing
for me
to be
your
festivity

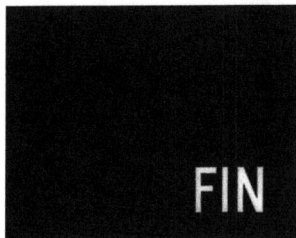

FIN

.

EPILOGUE

// you told me your father asked you
how you could love someone like me
and i replied by thinking

how could you not

// you said the heart
wants what it wants

l'amour existe

// i wonder
about the time i smoked a cigarette at de gaulle
& dreamt my life away on the flight to rome
to come & see you

a colt was my passport
the bad sleep well

// i am waiting

you're always waiting
intimidation isn't an honorable forte

essuie tes larmes

// i was hiding in a mist of vague promises
how was i to believe in my miracles
if you didn't believe in them yourself

// you asked me if i was afraid to be alone

my flesh is afraid
but i'm not

// my world exists
if only for myself

a law of effect

i'm not the type
to reach sovereignty
by popular favor

yet within all of this
futile wandering

i know where i'm going

// i'm a keen lover
& an affectionate

i besieged you
with these characteristics

// i've since
made a name for myself

// i'm cold
sitting by the fireplace
with a bottle of salers
watching the snowstorm

// my view for
the end of the world

la fin du monde